NATIONAL GEOGRAPHIC

Go for the Gold

PATHFINDER EDITION

By Ruth Kassinger and Shirleyann Costigan

CONTENTS

Gold feu

BY
Ruth Kassinger

Gold. People moved mountains to find it. Armies conquered faraway countries to control it. Find out how this glittering, shimmering metal has shaped history.

Don't touch that! It will make you crazy! Bill Adair ignored his boss's warning. He was 19, and it was the first night of his new job at the museum. He opened the dusty box and touched the thin layers of gold foil that lay inside. With that one touch, he caught gold fever. Forty years later, there seems to be no cure in sight.

Adair has devoted his life's work to gold. He has covered thousands of picture frames in gold, he has perched on rooftops to gild, or cover, the domes of buildings, and he has put gold leaf on walls, ceilings, and even statues of winged horses. What drives him to do this? Gold's glittering beauty.

Born in Earth

The gold Adair loves so much formed deep in Earth billions of years ago. Scientists believe that volcanoes may have heated underground water, which melted the gold. Liquid gold then flowed with the water through the cracks between rocks, and the shiny yellow metal cooled and hardened. In some places, the new **veins** of gold reached close to Earth's surface.

At the surface, the rushing water wore away the rock below, and over time, a vein of gold showed through, revealing the treasure. Tiny gold nuggets broke loose and settled at the bottom of the stream, and there they'd lie, waiting to be discovered, and discovered they were.

About 5,000 years ago, people found bits of beautiful gold in Egypt, and it didn't take long for them to catch gold fever. Since that time, gold has been discovered at different times all around the world, and with each new discovery, the same fever spikes. And each time the fever rises, the love of gold drives people to do almost anything. Let's look at some golden moments in history.

Old Money: This gold coin is more than 2,000 years old. It shows a chariot on one side.

The Fever Spreads

Egypt, 3,000 B.C.E. The pharaohs of Egypt surrounded themselves with gold. They ruled from golden thrones and gilded their chariots with gold. They wore gold crowns and gold jewelry, and they even buried their mummies wearing golden masks on their faces.

The pharaohs' hunger for gold grew and grew, and soon, small bits of easy-to-find gold were not enough to satisfy them. They wanted to follow veins of gold, deeper and deeper into Earth, but gold mining was dangerous work.

Miners used fires to crack the rocks, and the heat was fierce. Poisonous fumes filled the air, and the tunnels were so narrow that miners had to lie on their backs to navigate them. Small rocks fell on them, or large rocks crushed them. The pharaohs had to force slaves to do this risky job. Often, the slaves were captured in war and brought from faraway places to work in the mines.

Egypt traded its gold for valuable items from other countries, such as precious wood from Lebanon and horses from Babylonia. Jewelry and other golden objects traveled along the Silk Road, which was a series of trade routes stretching from Egypt all the way to China. Gold was the one thing everyone wanted, and that's how gold and gold fever spread.

Gold Coins

Turkey, 560 B.C.E. King Croesus ruled ancient Lydia, which is now western Turkey, and he played an important part in spreading gold fever. He came up with a new idea: to **mint,** or make, coins made of pure gold.

The coins made buying and selling much easier. Gold was the perfect metal to use because it lasts a long time and it's rare, so it's worth a lot. Gold is also soft, for a metal, so people could mold gold into shapes. That's just what Croesus did. He created coins that were the same size, weight, and value. The coins had a lion and a bull stamped on them.

Persia attacked Lydia, and Croesus lost his kingdom. But his golden money idea had already spread across the world, bringing gold fever with it.

Ancient Art. *Bill Adair caught gold fever when he was a teenager. Now he puts gold leaf on picture frames.*

Famous Face. *This gold mask was found on King Tut's mummy.*

Crowning Touch. *This crown belonged to a nomadic princess. She could fold it flat for quick travel.*

Gold in the Americas

South America, 1500s In the 1500s, word of an ancient **ceremony** spread across Europe. The story was told like this: *The Muisca king glittered as brightly as the sun because he had fine gold dust covering his whole body. He stood on a raft, piles of sparkling gold at his feet. At the center of the lake, he dropped the gold into the water, and then he dove in with a splash to wash the gold off his body. This would satisfy Muisca's god.*

Gold hunters asked: Did the golden man have a golden city? The story grew. This city, they thought, had streets paved with gold. They called it El Dorado. Gold fever had struck again.

As a result, Spanish explorers raced to South America. They searched for El Dorado, but they had no luck. But it wasn't all bad news—at least for the explorers—they discovered many South American people had gold. They had golden jewelry and art, and the explorers wanted that gold badly. So they killed or captured many thousands of people just to get it.

Atahualpa was an Inca leader, known as the Sun King. In 1532, Spanish gold hunter Francisco Pizarro found the Sun King's city. Pizarro came with 300 soldiers. The Sun King welcomed Pizarro and his men with music, but when Pizarro gave a signal, his soldiers fired their guns, shot 2,000 men, and captured the king. Pizarro said he'd set the king free in exchange for an entire roomful of gold. Pizarro got his gold, and yet he broke his promise and killed the Sun King. Pizarro would do anything for gold.

California, 1848 In 1848, a man saw flecks of gold in a stream in California. "GOLD MINE FOUND!" screamed a newspaper headline. The tiny flecks changed the United States forever because gold fever took over the whole country.

Tens of thousands of Americans dropped everything they were doing and headed west in search of fortune. They left their families, moved rocks, dug in mud, and waded in freezing streams. Some got hurt or sick, while others got lucky and found gold. The gold seekers kept coming, hoping they'd be next to strike it rich.

Gold's Global Grip

Worldwide, 2009 Today, finding gold is harder than ever. In most mines, workers find specks of gold so small that forty of them can fit in the period at the end of this sentence. Miners have to dig up 30 tons of rock just to find enough gold for one ring. But mining has left gashes in Earth, and the holes are so big, they can be seen from space! In 1990, gold was discovered in a volcano on an island in Indonesia. Now, the volcano has disappeared because miners have taken it apart, rock by rock.

The work in a gold mine still can be deadly, just as it was for Egyptian slaves. Today, many miners use a dangerous liquid called mercury to separate gold from rock, which can poison people and the environment.

Even so, the desire for gold keeps growing. In 2007, people around the world bought 2,500 tons (5 million pounds) of gold jewelry!

Today, gold is in demand for more than its shimmering beauty—it's used in computers, cell phones, and telescopes. Astronauts wear **visors** coated with a thin layer of gold because it protects them from the sun's strong rays. Doctors are studying ways that gold might help them fight cancer.

The ancient Egyptians may never have dreamed of using gold in these ways. Many years separate the pharoahs from today's miners, scientists, and artists, like Bill Adair. Yet one thing unites them all: gold fever.

Wordwise

ceremony: special actions and words used to celebrate an important event

mint: to make, or manufacture, coins

vein: narrow layer of mineral that forms in the crack of a rock

visor: shield on the front of a helmet that protects the face

Buried Treasure. *These gold-plated arms were found in a burial site in Peru. Today, Peru is one of the world's biggest producers of gold.*

Golden God. *The Incas called gold "the sweat of the sun." They used gold to make this image of a sun god.*

Sun Shield. *This is a model of an astronaut's helmet. A thin layer of gold protects the astronaut from possible damage caused by the sun's bright rays.*

It sparkles and glows, and it has dazzled people for thousands of years. But why is gold really so valuable? For one thing, it is strong and lasts a long time. Gold is also easily shaped. And gold is rare. In all history, only 161,000 tons of gold have been mined. That's enough to fit into just two large swimming pools. No wonder people find it so special!

Even as gold becomes harder to find, people are discovering new ways to use it. Here are some of the things that are now made with gold.

ELECTRONICS

Gold transfers heat and electricity well. For this reason, it is often used inside electronic devices and computers. The gold wires inside many circuit boards are about the size of a human hair.

JEWELRY

Has anybody ever told you a piece of jewelry was made of "pure gold"? If they did, they were probably mistaken because gold in its purest state is considered too soft to be made into jewelry. Today, most jewelers mix harder metals with gold, so the gold rings and necklaces stay scratch-free.

SPACE TECHNOLOGY

Gold does not break down easily, so it is valuable for use in spacecrafts. Nearly 41 kilograms (90 pounds) of gold were used in the U.S. Columbia space shuttle, shown here.

COLUMBIA SPACE SHUTTLE/NASA

© BEN EDWARDS/GETTY IMAGES

DENTISTRY

Gold is a metal, and it is relatively soft, so it can be shaped to fit on teeth. People have used gold in teeth for thousands of years. Here, a gold crown is being fitted onto a model, and later it will be attached to a real tooth.

HOW GOLD IS USED
(in tons for 2008)

| BUYING & SELLING GOLD TO MAKE MONEY (1183.4) | DENTISTRY (55.9) | OTHER INDUSTRIAL USES (86.9) | ELECTRONICS (292.7) | JEWELRY (2186.7) |

Source: World Gold Council

ISTOCKPHOTO.COM

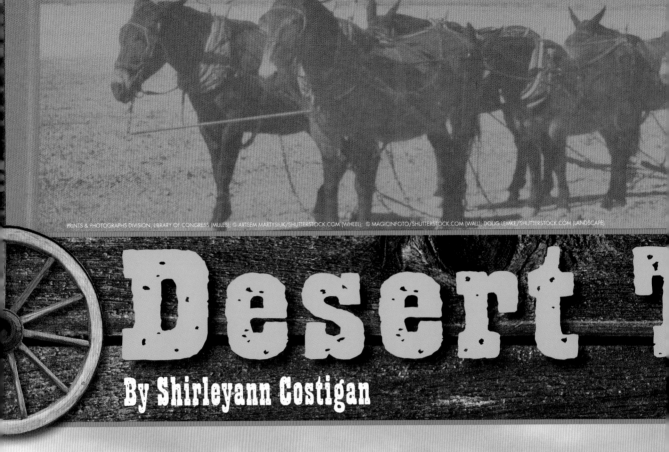

Desert

By Shirleyann Costigan

Past and Present. A twenty-mule team hauls borax out of Death Valley (top). The moon rises over the colorful rocks of Zabriskie Point (bottom).

reasure

In the past, pioneers came to California's Death Valley in search of gold. Now that the gold is gone, people are finding a different kind of treasure here—one that's all around them!

Death Valley

Death Valley deserves its name. It is a sunburnt land of salt flats, bad water, and scorching sand. It is an eerie place where people get lost and are never heard from again. The valley is the burning heart of a much larger desert called the Mojave (moh HAH vee).

This parched place is the hottest, driest spot in North America, with summer temperatures that may rise to over 49° Celsisus (120° Fahrenheit). The valley gets less than five centimeters (two inches) of rain a year, and in some years, no rain falls on the valley at all.

It may seem that no one could ever survive here. Yet people have lived in this valley for thousands of years. Let's meet some of these people and explore their stories.

At Home in the Heat

Death Valley has not always been a desert. It was once a lake. The climate was much wetter, and the land nearby was rich with life.

The valley was still a lake when the first Native Americans arrived. That was about 10,000 years ago. About 1,000 years ago, the ancestors of today's Timbisha Shoshone people came to the valley. Over time, the climate changed. Temperatures rose, and less rain fell. The lake dried up, and only a few freshwater springs remained in the foothills, mountains, and valley.

The Timbisha adapted as Death Valley grew hotter and drier. They moved their villages close to the springs, and they learned to survive on what they could find in the desert.

Jackrabbits, quail, and bighorn sheep provided meat, and people learned to grind up pods from mesquite trees and make small cakes to eat. Branches and twigs became the walls and roofs of open, airy homes.

During the hottest season, the Timbisha moved into the mountains, where the climate was cooler. The rest of the year, though, they lived in the valley. The Timbisha lived this unchanging life for centuries, and they respected the desert and cared for it. Then, in 1849, **pioneers** arrived from the East.

The Lost Pioneers

The first group of pioneers was lost, while trying to find a shortcut to the California gold fields. They had already spent two months crossing a desert in Nevada, and now not only were their wagons breaking down, but they were near starvation as well.

On Christmas Eve, they found a spring near the Timbisha settlements, where they made camp and talked about what to do. One of the pioneers, William Lewis Manly, wrote about the experience.

"We all felt pretty much downhearted. Our civilized provisions were getting so scarce that all must be saved for the women and children, and the men must get along some way on ox meat alone. It was decided not a scrap of anything that would sustain life must go to waste, so the blood, hide, and intestines were all prepared in some way for food.

"This meeting lasted till late at night. If some of them had lost their minds I should not have been surprised, for hunger swallows all other feelings. A man in a starving condition is a savage."

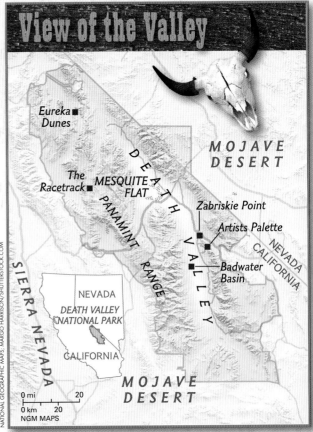

View of the Valley

Eureka Dunes

MOJAVE DESERT

The Racetrack

MESQUITE FLAT

DEATH VALLEY

PANAMINT RANGE

SIERRA NEVADA

Zabriskie Point

Artists Palette

NEVADA

CALIFORNIA

Badwater Basin

NEVADA

DEATH VALLEY NATIONAL PARK

CALIFORNIA

MOJAVE DESERT

0 mi   20
0 km   20
NGM MAPS

NATIONAL GEOGRAPHIC MAPS; MARGO HARRISON/SHUTTERSTOCK.COM

Long Walk

The pioneers decided to split into several groups, each one having its own plan. Manly's group began a long walk toward the mountains.

The group faced new challenges. Because there was little for the oxen to eat, the animals grew weak and could no longer pull the pioneers' wagons.

The pioneers had no choice: They left the wagons behind, and they killed several oxen for food. Finally, the pioneers crossed over the Panamint Range. They had made it through Death Valley.

The flat, dry plains of the Mojave were the worst part of their journey. Luckily, it had been a wet winter, and puddles of melted snow and ice provided water. Without that, all of them would have died. "We were lucky in our misfortune," Manly wrote. Amazingly enough, the whole group survived the Mojave trek.

You might think the pioneers' experience would have kept other people from following, but it didn't. Newcomers came with only mules and pickaxes, and they, too, were searching for gold.

© THOMAS HALLSTEIN/ALAMY

Four-Legged Food. *Native Americans hunted bighorn sheep and painted them on rocks.*

Thirsty Valley. *From Zabriskie Point, you can see the tough landscape that people have faced in Death Valley.*

© CHRISTIAN BEEK/AGEFOTOSTOCK

13

The Fortune Hunters

Valuable **ores** lay hidden beneath Death Valley. These treasures included gold and silver. When miners gave up on the gold fields in other parts of California, many came to the desert.

Most mining settlements followed the same predictable pattern. First came the **prospectors.** They searched for gold deposits. When they made a **strike,** they staked a claim. Then they either worked the claim themselves or sold it.

Word got out about the strike: *Gold! Gold!* More prospectors came. Miners poured into the area. They set up mining camps. Soon the camps became towns. More people came. They built banks, hospitals, restaurants, hotels, and a jail. The towns became cities.

Everything in a mining town depended on the local mine. Sooner or later, though, it dried up, which meant there was no more gold. Everyone left and the place became a ghost town. It was all over.

This pattern repeated itself many times in Death Valley. During the late 1800s and early 1900s, mining towns sprouted up everywhere. They had colorful names like Bullfrog, Skidoo, Ballarat, and Rhyolite.

Twenty-Mule Teams

Miners came to Death Valley for more than gold. Some came to mine a kind of salt, which was used to make a substance called borax. Borax was then used to make glass, ceramics, and cleaning products.

In the 1880s, mining borax salts became big business, but it also became a big challenge. Carrying huge loads of borax out of the valley wasn't easy.

William T. Coleman solved the problem. He used twenty-mule teams to carry borax from his factory in Death Valley to the railroad line. Actually, it was eighteen mules and two horses, but people tend to forget about the horses. Each team pulled two full wagons, plus a water tank. Imagine hauling that huge load across a burning desert!

Tough Job

Between 1883 and 1889, mule teams hauled more than 9 million kilograms (20 million pounds) of borax out of the valley. The route ran 265 kilometers (165 miles) out of Death Valley, and one round-trip took twenty days. It was a hard journey for both the mules and the men who drove them.

Driving a twenty-mule team took talent and courage. One bad step, and the team could run the wagons into a mountain or off a cliff. The driver cracked a long whip to get the mules' attention, but mostly, he used just his voice.

A good mule driver didn't shout, though—at least that's how Tex Ewell remembered it. Only bad drivers raised their voices. Ewell said that when a skilled driver spoke, "a mule knew he wasn't fooling" and obeyed.

Death Valley Today

Today, Death Valley is a national park, and in fact, it is the largest U.S. national park outside Alaska. There is plenty for tourists to see.

Some of the favorite natural sites include Badwater Basin, the spectacular Eureka Dunes, and the rainbow-colored clay at Artists Palette. These are places that never change.

Well, almost never. There is a strange place called the Racetrack, where rocks move around mysteriously, carving long tracks in the mud. But no one has ever seen it happen, so exactly what takes place remains a puzzle.

All that remains of the mining days are ghost towns and tombstones. Through it all, the Timbisha Shoshone have continued to live here. This valley is still their home forever, and for them, it is a valley of life.

A Gift for Gold. *Shorty Harris, pictured at right, was Death Valley's most famous gold hunter. He made a big strike in 1904.*

Prized Park. *Death Valley once lured miners, but today, it draws nearly a million tourists every year.*

Wordwise

ore: substance mined for its value

pioneer: one of the first people to move to a new place

prospector: person who searches a place for gold or other valuable material

strike: discovery of something valuable

The Search for Gold

It's time to dig deeper to find out what you learned about the search for gold.

 Picture the formation of gold. Why do people often find gold in streams?

 How did "gold fever" affect South America? How did it affect North America?

 How did "gold fever" change the history of Death Valley?

 Why do people visit Death Valley today? What treasures do they find there?

 Why do you think people value gold so much?